WHAT MAKES YOU THINK YOU'RE HAPPY?

WHAT MAKES YOU THINK YOU'RE HAPPY?

Cartoons from *Snoopy*

by Charles M. Schulz

An Owl Book

Henry Holt and Company / New York

Originally published as *Snoopy* by Holt, Rinehart and Winston
in 1973. Published in an expanded edition under the title
What Makes You Think You're Happy? by Holt, Rinehart and Winston
in 1976, and included strips from *You're Out of Your Mind,
Charlie Brown!*, published by Holt, Rinehart and Winston in 1959.

Library of Congress Catalog Card Number: 90-81563

ISBN: 0-8050-1483-7 (An Owl Book: pbk.)

Henry Holt books are available at special discounts
for bulk purchases for sales promotions, premiums,
fund-raising, or educational use. Special editions
or book excerpts can also be created to specifications.
For details contact:
Special Sales Director, Henry Holt and Company, Inc.,
115 West 18th Street, New York, New York 10011.

First Owl Book Edition—1990

Printed in the United States of America

Recognizing the importance of preserving the written word,
Henry Holt and Company, Inc., by policy, prints all of its
first editions on acid-free paper. ∞
1 3 5 7 9 10 8 6 4 2

LISTEN TO THIS DEFINITION IN THE DICTIONARY..

"dog (dog) I. *n* 1. Domestic quadruped. 2. Andiron. II *vt.* Follow as a dog."

OH, HO HO HO HO HO!! A DOMESTIC QUADRUPED! WOW! AN ANDIRON! HA HA HA HA!

I MIGHT AS WELL GO HOME AND GO TO BED.. THIS COULD TURN OUT TO BE A VERY BAD DAY...

CLUMP!

YIPE!

REAL ALLIGATORS DON'T BITE THEIR OWN TONGUES...

SNOOPY, PRETENDING THAT YOU'RE AN ALLIGATOR DOESN'T **MAKE** YOU ONE, YOU KNOW...

WHY CAN'T YOU BE SATISFIED WITH JUST BEING A DOG?

BE HAPPY WITH THE THINGS YOU HAVE! BE HAPPY WITH WHAT YOU ARE!!

YOU DUMB DOG

PTUI!

SCHULZ

REMEMBER THE ALAMO!!

IF YOU'RE GOING TO LEARN TO SWIM, LUCY, WHY DON'T YOU BEGIN WITH THE 'DOG-PADDLE'?

IT'S VERY EASY TO LEARN, AND IT'S THE WAY ALL DOGS SWIM.

WITH A FEW STUPID EXCEPTIONS, OF COURSE..

ZIP!

SCHULZ

BOY, I GOTTA CUT THIS OUT..

THOSE COLD SNOWBALLS MAKE MY GOLD FILLINGS ACHE!

SCHULZ

DON'T YOU RUFFLE YOUR FUR AT ME! PUT IT DOWN!

PUT IT **ALL** DOWN!

☆ SIGH ☆

SCHULZ

"IN THE FALL OF THE YEAR ANIMALS ARE HARD AT WORK MAKING THEIR PREPARATIONS FOR WINTER.."

"THIS, OF COURSE, IS NOT TRUE OF **ALL** ANIMALS.."

"SOME GO MERRILY ON THEIR WAY DEPENDING ON MAN AND NATURE SOMEHOW TO SUSTAIN THEM."

SCHULZ

I JUST CAN'T TURN DOWN A BEGGING DOG..

SCHULZ

WHERE ARE THOSE MARBLES?

I **DEMAND** TO KNOW WHO TOOK THOSE MARBLES!

I JUST BETTER NOT CATCH THE GUY WHO'S GOT THOSE MARBLES!

SCHULZ

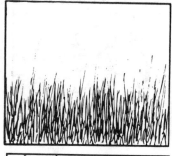

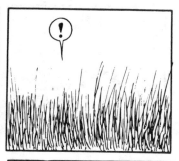

AAK!

SNOOPY COULD NEVER BE A HUNTING DOG... TALL WEEDS GIVE HIM CLAUSTROPHOBIA!

"CLAUSTROPHOBIA, AN ABNORMAL FEAR OF BEING IN AN ENCLOSED PLACE"

YOU'D THINK THERE'D BE SOME MENTION OF "WEED-CLAUSTROPHOBIA", WOULDN'T YOU?

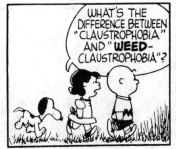

STOP IT! STOP IT THIS INSTANT! WITH ALL THE TROUBLE THERE IS IN THIS WORLD, YOU HAVE NO RIGHT TO BE SO HAPPY!!

SHE'S RIGHT...I'VE GOT TO START ACTING MORE SENSIBLE...

...TOMORROW!

SCHULZ

I THOUGHT I TOLD YOU TO STOP THAT DANCING?! YOU HAVE NO RIGHT TO BE SO HAPPY!!! NOW, STOP IT! DO YOU HEAR ME?!

SCHULZ

THE FLOOD WATERS ARE RISING!!

I COULD NEVER BE SNEAKY ..IT'S TOO HARD ON THE EYES!

SCHULZ

SO YOU WON'T COME DOWN, EH?

THEN YOU KNOW WHAT WE'RE GOING TO DO? WE'RE GOING TO IGNORE YOU !!!

RATS! I CAN'T STAND BEING IGNORED!

SCHULZ

OH, GO AWAY! I HAVEN'T GOT ANYTHING!

THAT'S THE ONLY DOG I KNOW WHO CAN SMELL SOMEONE JUST **THINKING** ABOUT FOOD!

PHOOEY! I CAN THINK OF NOTHING MORE REPULSIVE THAN BEING AN ANTEATER!

EXCUSE ME.. I THINK SOMEBODY'S WATER DISH IS EMPTY

SNOOPY, I'VE GOT SOMETHING TO SAY TO YOU!

NOW, YOU SIT DOWN, AND LISTEN TO ME!

YOU SIT HERE, AND LISTEN TO WHAT I HAVE TO SAY!

AND DON'T ROLL UP YOUR EARS!!

THOSE DUMB KIDS! I'LL BET IF I WERE A POLAR BEAR, THEY'D NEVER THROW SNOWBALLS AT ME!

IF I WERE A POLAR BEAR I'D WALK RIGHT OVER TO THEM, AND I'D..

HERE COMES THE BIG WHITE POLAR BEAR..

HERE COMES THE BIG WHITE POLAR BEAR SNEAKING UP ON THE ESKIMO...

HOW IN THE WORLD COULD ANYONE EVER EAT A WHOLE ESKIMO?

IT'S EASY FOR HIM TO BE SO HAPPY..HE DOESN'T HAVE ANY WORRIES!

WELL, WHAT ABOUT YOURSELF? WHAT IN THE WORLD DO **YOU** HAVE TO WORRY ABOUT?!

BOY I DIDN'T THINK LINUS WAS EVER GOING TO LEAVE!

HE NEVER SEEMS TO KNOW WHEN TO GO HOME..

HE'LL STICK AROUND UNTIL THE LAST DOG IS HUNG..

..IF YOU'LL PARDON THE EXPRESSION..

CAN YOU TAKE DICTATION?

GOOD GRIEF! I THINK I FROZE MY STOMACH!

THUMP

WELL, **THAT** SURE WAS A DIRTY TRICK!

SCHULZ

YOU'LL NOTICE, LINUS, THAT YOU HAVE **TWO** EARS BUT ONLY **ONE** MOUTH..

THAT'S BECAUSE LISTENING IS MORE IMPORTANT THAN TALKING... TWO EYES AND ONE NOSE MEANS THAT SEEING IS MORE IMPORTANT THAN SMELLING...

FOUR LEGS, I GUESS, MEANS THAT RUNNING IS THE MOST IMPORTANT OF ALL...

SCHULZ

INCREDIBLE!

CHARLIE BROWN, WHAT DOES IT MEAN TO 'RUB SOMEBODY THE WRONG WAY'?

WELL,...TO...UH...IT MEANS TO... UH...TO...UH...HMM...IT...UH...

WAIT A MINUTE...I'LL DEMONSTRATE..

OH, YES...I UNDERSTAND...THAT'S WHAT I THOUGHT IT MEANT

I'VE HEARD THAT A LOT OF CROOKS HAVE TINY EYES...

OH, THAT'S TRUE...YOU CAN'T TRUST ANYONE WHO HAS SMALL EYES...

LET'S SEE **YOUR** EYES, SNOOPY...

HE'S RIGHT... I **DO** HAVE A FUZZY FACE!

MMM!

I LIKE YOU, SNOOPY... I LIKE YOU BECAUSE YOU HAVE SUCH A WARM, FUZZY FACE!

PEANUT BUTTER!

HE LOVES PEOPLE!

I GOTTA START
LEARNING SOME
NEW STEPS..

THE WORST THING A PERSON
CAN DO IS WASTE HIS LIFE
HANGING AROUND STREET CORNERS!

HAVE YOU EVER SEEN A PENGUIN, CHARLIE BROWN?

I'VE SEEN PICTURES OF THEM..

THEY'RE SORT OF A FUNNY LOOKING BIRD.. THEY WALK KIND OF STRAIGHT, AND THEY LOOK SORT OF...WELL...

YEAH..THAT'S RIGHT... SORT OF LIKE THAT..

THAT'S THE ONLY PENGUIN IN THE WORLD WITH LONG BLACK EARS!

REAL PENGUINS DON'T GET COLD FEET!

SCHULZ

CALYPSO..

GOOD GRIEF!

SCHULZ